Christmas
Party

This book is perfect for:

 Family game nights (gather around the Christmas tree!)

🎄 Holiday road trips (because Santa's sleigh isn't always available)

🎁 Christmas parties (let's make it a holiday to remember!)

🎉 Anytime you want to have a little holiday fun!

It's easy to play: just read a question, think about your answer, and share it with your family or friends. You might even learn something new about each other—like who secretly wishes they were an elf!

So, what are you waiting for? Grab your family, your holiday spirit, and maybe a cookie (or two).

Let's dive into a world of Christmas magic, laughter, and fun!

Are you ready to play? Let's go—Santa is waiting!

Simple Rules
for Families & Kids

Get Ready:

Gather everyone in a cozy spot, like around the Christmas tree. One person starts as the reader and reads a question aloud to the group.

How to Play:

Take turns answering the Would You Rather question. Pick one of the two options—no explanation needed unless you want to!

Go around the group until everyone has had a turn.

Make It Fun (Optional):

- **Voting:** After everyone answers, the group can vote on the funniest or most creative answer.
- **Snowflake Points:** The person with the most votes gets 1 "snowflake point." The player with the most points at the end wins!
- **Silly Challenge:** If someone refuses to choose, they must do a fun challenge like singing a Christmas song or pretending to be Santa!

4

Simple Rules
for Families & Kids

For Younger Kids:

Explain the choices to make sure they understand, and cheer for every answer to keep it fun and encouraging.

End the Game:

When you're done playing, name the person with the funniest or most creative answers as the "Christmas Fun Champion!" 🎄👑

LET'S START!

6

ROUND 1
Eat & drink

WOULD YOU RATHER?

**DRINK HOT
CHOCOLATE
WITH DOUBLE
MARSHMALLOWS**

OR

**DRINK
RICH
EGGNOG**

8

WOULD YOU RATHER?

EAT
GINGERBREAD
ALL WEEK

OR

EAT
PEPPERMINT
CANDY
EVERY DAY

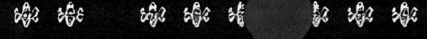

WOULD YOU RATHER?

ROAST CHICKEN FOR CHRISTMAS DINNER

OR

BACON FOR CHRISTMAS DINNER

WOULD YOU RATHER?

**HAVE
ONE
GIANT
CAKE**

OR

**HAVE
100 TINY
COOKIES**

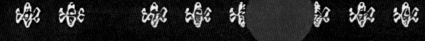

WOULD YOU RATHER?

EAT
BURNT
COOKIES

OR

DRINK OVERLY
SWEET HOT
CHOCOLATE

WOULD YOU RATHER?

EAT A
BOWL OF
CHRISTMAS
SALAD

OR

EAT A
PLATE OF
COLD MEAT

WOULD YOU RATHER?

MAKE A
GIANT CAKE
FOR THE
FAMILY

OR

DECORATE
CAKES FOR
EACH
PERSON

WOULD YOU RATHER?

A TABLE FULL OF
TRADITIONAL
CHRISTMAS FOOD

OR

JUST
SNACKS

WOULD YOU RATHER?

EAT MUFFINS
WITH FILLING

OR

EAT MUFFINS
WITHOUT FILLING

WOULD YOU RATHER?

EAT CHRISTMAS
TREE COOKIES

OR

EAT CHRISTMAS
REINDEER COOKIES

Winner

ROUND 1

IS

....

ROUND 2
Decoration

WOULD YOU RATHER?

DECORATE
A TALL
CHRISTMAS
TREE

OR

HANG
FLASHING
LIGHTS
AROUND
HOUSE

WOULD YOU RATHER?

MAKE A
WREATH BY
HAND

OR

MAKE A
SNOWMAN
OUT OF
PAPER

WOULD YOU RATHER?

DECORATE
YOUR TREE
WITH
CANDIES

 OR

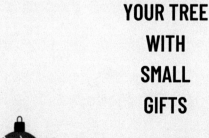

DECORATE
YOUR TREE
WITH
SMALL
GIFTS

WOULD YOU RATHER?

PUT A BIG
SHINY STAR
ON TOP OF
YOUR TREE

OR

PUT AN
ELEGANT BOW
ON TOP OF
YOUR TREE

WOULD YOU RATHER?

HAVE A
HOUSE THAT
SPARKLES

OR

HAVE A
MINIMALIST
HOUSE

WOULD YOU RATHER?

USE
HANDMADE
CHILDREN'S
DECORATIONS

OR

USE FANCY
AND
EXPENSIVE
ONES

WOULD YOU RATHER?

HANG 100 SMALL
STOCKINGS
AROUND THE
FIREPLACE

OR

JUST ONE
GIANT
STOCKING

WOULD YOU RATHER?

A WALL OF LETTERS TO SANTA

OR

A CHRISTMAS WALL FILLED WITH FAMILY PHOTOS

WOULD YOU RATHER?

DECORATE DOOR IN YOUR HOUSE WITH A MINI WREATH

OR

HANG SOME LITTLE CHRISTMAS BELLS

WOULD YOU RATHER?

MAKE DECORATIONS FROM FOOD LIKE COOKIES, CANDIES

OR

MAKE DECORATIONS FROM YARN

Winner

ROUND 2

IS

....

ROUND 3
Ho Ho Holiday

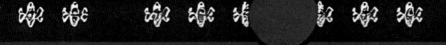

WOULD YOU RATHER?

BUILD A GIANT SNOWMAN

OR

JOIN AN ENDLESS SNOWBALL FIGHT

WOULD YOU RATHER?

HAVE A
CHRISTMAS
WITHOUT
SNOW

OR

HAVE A
CHRISTMAS
WITHOUT
PRESENTS

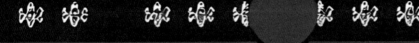

WOULD YOU RATHER?

GO GIFT SHOPPING ON CHRISTMAS EVE

OR

SING CHRISTMAS CAROLS IN THE STREET

WOULD YOU RATHER?

WRAP
100
GIFTS

OR

OPEN
100
GIFTS

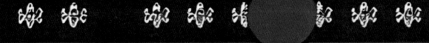

WOULD YOU RATHER?

SKI DOWN A HIGH HILL

OR

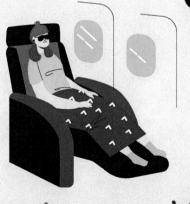

SIT IN A WARM CABIN ALL DAY

WOULD YOU RATHER?

ATTEND A COZY CHRISTMAS PARTY

OR

ATTEND A SNOWY OUTDOOR PARTY

WOULD YOU RATHER?

SPEND CHRISTMAS WITH YOUR FAMILY

OR

SPEND CHRISTMAS WITH YOUR FRIENDS

WOULD YOU RATHER?

SPEND CHRISTMAS AT THE NORTH POLE

OR

SPEND CHRISTMAS IN A TROPICAL SEA

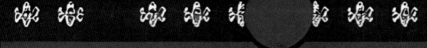

WOULD YOU RATHER?

COOKING FOR
CHRISTMAS
DINNER

OR

WASHING
DISHES FOR
CHRISTMAS
DINNER

WOULD YOU RATHER?

BUILD A
SNOWMAN

OR

BUILD A
SNOW
CASTLE

Winner

ROUND 3

IS

....

ROUND 4
Santa's Workshop

WOULD YOU RATHER?

WEAR A
SANTA SUIT

OR

WEAR A
REINDEER
SUIT

WOULD YOU RATHER?

BE SANTA'S
ASSISTANT

OR

BE RUDOLPH 'S
BEST FRIEND

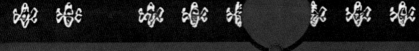

WOULD YOU RATHER?

HAVE A MAGIC
PAIR OF SHOES
THAT TAKE YOU
ANYWHERE

OR

HAVE A JACKET
THAT KEEPS
YOU FROM
FREEZING

WOULD YOU RATHER?

LISTEN TO TRADITIONAL CHRISTMAS MUSIC

OR

LISTEN TO MODERN SONGS

WOULD YOU RATHER?

SEE THE
REAL
SANTA

OR

RIDE THE
RED-NOSED
REINDEER
FOR ONCE

WOULD YOU RATHER?

WEAR
COLORFUL
CHRISTMAS
SOCKS

OR

WEAR
LIGHT UP
SOCKS
WHEN YOU
WALK

WOULD YOU RATHER?

**WEAR A
SANTA HAT**

OR

**WEAR
A REINDEER
ANTLER
HEADBAND**

WOULD YOU RATHER?

GO TO ALL THE CHRISTMAS EVENTS IN A CHRISTMAS PAJAMA

OR

GO TO ALL THE CHRISTMAS EVENTS IN A GORGEOUS EVENING GOWN

WOULD YOU RATHER?

WEAR A PAIR OF WOOL GLOVES

OR

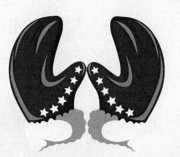

WEAR A PAIR OF LEATHER GLOVES

WOULD YOU RATHER?

WEAR A PAIR
OF CHRISTMAS
TREE GLASSES

OR

WEAR A PAIR
OF REINDEER
GLASSES

Winner

ROUND 4

IS

....

ROUND 5
Magic Christmas

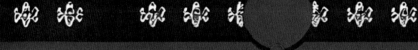

WOULD YOU RATHER?

SPEND A DAY IN THE ELVES' TOY FACTORY

OR

EXPLORE THE ICE CAVE WHERE SANTA LIVES

WOULD YOU RATHER?

RECEIVE
A SMALL
GIFT

OR

RECEIVE
A LARGE
GIFT

WOULD YOU RATHER?

RECEIVE
GIFTS ALL
MONTH LONG

OR

RECEIVE
SPECIAL
GIFT ON
CHRISTMAS
DAY

WOULD YOU RATHER?

ATTEND A
CHRISTMAS PARTY
WITH SANTA AND
THE ELVES

OR

WITH FAIRY TALE
CHARACTERS

WOULD YOU RATHER?

GO SKIING ON A MAGICAL
SNOW-COVERED
MOUNTAIN

OR

EXPLORE A
MAGICAL GLOWING
FOREST

WOULD YOU RATHER?

HAVE THE ABILITY
TO FLY UP INTO
THE SKY

OR

HAVE THE ABILITY
TO TURN SNOW
INTO ANY SHAPE
YOU WANT

WOULD YOU RATHER?

TRAVEL ACROSS
THE NORTH POLE
BY REINDEER
SLEIGH

OR

TRAVEL ACROSS
THE NORTH POLE
BY A MAGICAL
TRAIN

WOULD YOU RATHER?

ATTEND A
NORTH POLE
LIGHT FESTIVAL

OR

ATTEND AN
UNDERWATER
CHRISTMAS
PARTY

WOULD YOU RATHER?

GO ON AN ADVENTURE TO FIND THE LEGENDARY CHRISTMAS TREE

OR

EXPLORE A FORGOTTEN FAIRY TALE VILLAGE

WOULD YOU RATHER?

CREATE THE WORLD'S
LARGEST CHRISTMAS
TREE

OR

CREATE THE WORLD'S
MOST PERFECT
SNOWFLAKE

Winner

ROUND 5

IS

....

Winner

ALL ROUND

IS

....

WISHING YOU A

Merry Christmas

I HOPE SANTA IS GOOD TO YOU THIS YEAR!

THE END!

Christmas
Party

Ho, ho, ho! Welcome to the most fun-filled, giggle-packed Christmas game EVER! This is Would You Rather? Christmas Edition, a magical book full of silly, tricky, and downright hilarious questions about everything Christmas!

    Are you ready to let your imagination sparkle like the star on top of a Christmas tree? In this book, you'll get to decide between all kinds of fun and funny holiday situations. Would you rather ride in Santa's sleigh or have a snowball fight with a talking snowman? Wear a candy cane crown or eat only Christmas cookies for a whole week? There's no wrong answer—only lots of laughs and big smiles!

Conte

MW00890843

Round

Round

Round

Round

Round